Snakes on the Hunt

PYTHONS

Amy Austen

PowerKiDS press
New York

Published in 2017 by The Rosen Publishing Group, Inc.
29 East 21st Street, New York, NY 10010

First Edition

Editor: Caitie McAneney
Book Design: Mickey Harmon

Photo Credits: Cover (series logo) iLoveCoffeeDesign/Shutterstock.com; cover, pp. 1, 3, 4, 6, 8, 10, 12, 14, 16, 20, 22—24 (background) cla78/Shutterstock.com; cover (python), p. 22 Kuznetsov Alexey/Shutterstock.com; p. 5 Peerajit Dittain/Shutterstock.com; p. 7 (main) Sanne vd Berg Fotografie/Shutterstock.com; p. 7 (reticulated python) apple2499/Shutterstock.com; p. 7 (African rock python) Ryan M. Bolton/Shutterstock.com; p. 8 Paul Tessier/Shutterstock.com; pp. 9, 11, 21 Heiko Kiera/Shutterstock.com; p. 13 reptiles4all/Shutterstock.com; p. 15 Alta Oosthuizen/Shutterstock.com; p. 17 Alberto Loyo/Shutterstock.com; p. 19 Marek Velechovsky/Shutterstock.com.

Library of Congress Cataloging-in-Publication Data

Names: Austen, Amy, author.
Title: Pythons / Amy Austen.
Description: New York : PowerKids Press, [2017] | Series: Snakes on the hunt | Includes index.
Identifiers: LCCN 2016009958 | ISBN 9781499421989 (pbk.) | ISBN 9781499422009 (library bound) | ISBN 9781499421996 (6 pack)
Subjects: LCSH: Pythons–Juvenile literature.
Classification: LCC QL666.O67 A97 2017 | DDC 597.96/78–dc23
LC record available at http://lccn.loc.gov/2016009958

Manufactured in the United States of America

CPSIA Compliance Information: Batch #BS16PK: For Further Information contact Rosen Publishing, New York, New York at 1-800-237-9932

Contents

The Longest Snakes! 4
What's a Python? 6
A Python's Life 8
Pythons at Home 10
Powerful Python Senses 12
Python Defenses 14
The Predator's Menu 16
Hunting Prey 18
Are Pythons in Danger? 20
Protecting Pythons 22
Glossary 23
Index 24
Websites 24

The Longest Snakes!

Pythons are some of the longest, scariest snakes in the world. They're powerful predators that use their long bodies to squeeze their **prey** to death. This makes them **constrictors**.

There are about 30 **species** in the family Pythonidae, all of which are called pythons. The reticulated python holds the title for the longest snake in the world! The Burmese python and African rock python are also two of the longest snakes that exist.

Snake Bites

Pythons have a lot in common with anacondas. They're both constrictors.

This Burmese python has a colorful pattern on its skin. Some people keep these pythons as pets, but that's not safe!

What's a Python?

Imagine you're on a walk when, suddenly, you see a snake. How do you know if it's a python?

You can **identify** many pythons by their long bodies. Some species can grow to more than 30 feet (9.1 m) long! Burmese pythons can grow to around 23 feet (7 m) and weigh up to 200 pounds (90.7 kg). Pythons have sharp, curved teeth. However, unlike **venomous** snakes, they don't kill their prey with a bite.

Snake Bites

Some pythons have patterns on their skin that help them blend in with their surroundings. That's called camouflage.

Pythons come in many different colors. They can be brown, tan, gray, or yellowish brown.

A Python's Life

Pythons usually live alone. That makes them solitary animals. However, males and females come together to mate, or make babies. Burmese pythons can lay up to 100 eggs at a time!

Unlike many snakes, most python mothers stay with their eggs until they hatch, or break open. They curl around their pile of eggs. When it's cold, the mother "shivers," or makes small muscle movements. This keeps her eggs warm. When the eggs hatch, the young snakes leave the nest and start their life.

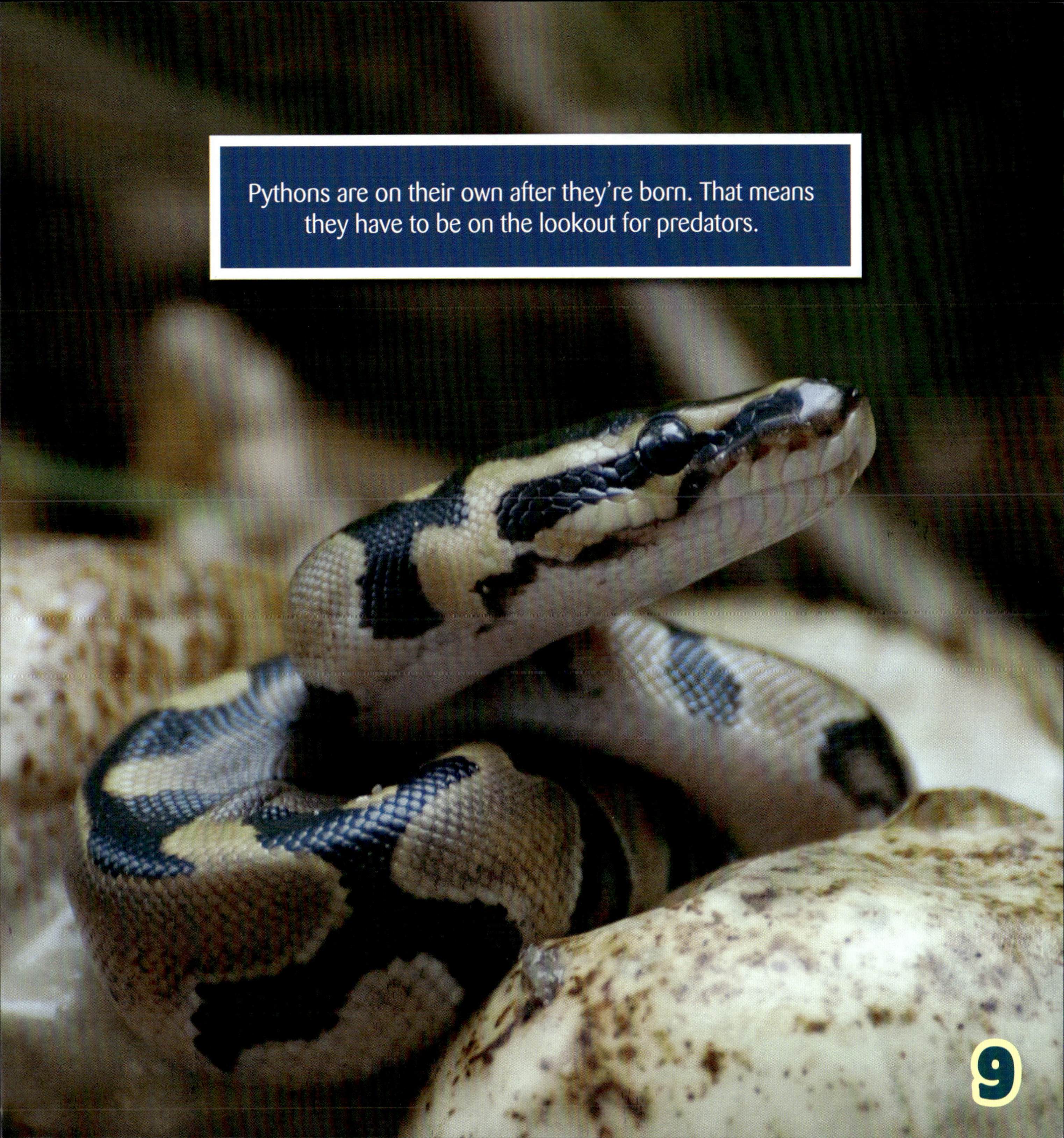

Pythons are on their own after they're born. That means they have to be on the lookout for predators.

Pythons at Home

Where can you find pythons? They live in Africa, Southeast Asia, and Australia. You can also find them in India and China.

Pythons can live in many different **habitats**. Some live in the rain forest, while others live on flat grasslands. Still others live in the woods or in swamps. Young, smaller pythons hang out in trees. Bigger pythons mostly stay on the ground. Pythons are even at home in the water! Like many snakes, they're great swimmers.

Snake Bites

Over the years, people have taken pythons out of their natural habitats. They brought pythons to the United States, Europe, and South America to sell as pets.

A Burmese python can stay underwater for up to 30 minutes at a time!

Powerful Python Senses

Pythons need to have great senses when they're on a hunt. They don't have the best sense of sight. Luckily, they have other senses to make up for it!

Each python has a special body part on the roof of its mouth called a Jacobson's organ. The python flicks its tongue out and collects a smell. Then, the tongue sends the smell to the Jacobson's organ, which identifies the smell. Pythons can also sense heat around them, which helps them find prey.

Snake Bites

Snakes feel vibrations, or small, quick movements, on the ground. That lets them know if prey is nearby.

Pythons "smell" with their tongue!

Python Defenses

Pythons are near the top of their food chain. That's because they have great **defenses**. The greatest defense for larger pythons is their size. Few predators want to attack one of the world's longest snakes! Another defense is the python's strength. If an enemy attacks, the python can give it a deadly squeeze.

Small pythons have fewer defenses. They are sometimes caught by crocodiles, large birds, large **mammals**, and lizards. If an animal is larger than a python, it might try to eat the smaller snake.

Can you think of any animal brave enough to battle a huge python?

The Predator's Menu

Pythons will eat nearly anything they can fit in their mouth. They eat birds, reptiles, and mammals.

The larger the snake, the larger its prey. Pythons hunt small animals, such as mice, and big animals, such as pigs and deer. They can even swallow a crocodile! Pythons can fit large animals in their mouth by stretching their jaw. The huge meal slips right down the python's throat. You can sometimes see the outline of a large animal in a python's body!

Snake Bites

It can take a python a long time to **digest** a big meal. That means it doesn't have to hunt for a while.

This python just ate a gazelle!

Hunting Prey

Pythons hunt by ambushing their prey. That means they wait for the animal to come along and then they strike by surprise. They're good at hiding from prey because their skin can blend into their surroundings. Pythons that hunt in water might hide their bodies underwater while keeping just their eyes above the surface to watch for prey.

Pythons strike quickly. They grab their prey and wind around it. Then, the python squeezes the animal tightly. This cuts off the animal's air and blood supply and kills it quickly.

This python has caught an unlucky mouse!

Are Pythons in Danger?

The python might be a mighty hunter in the wild, but it still faces danger. Many species are losing their habitat. As people cut down trees and build new structures, pythons and other animals lose their homes. Some pythons are killed for their skin, which is used to make purses and shoes. Others are taken from their homes to be sold as pets.

Keeping a python as a pet is usually unsafe for both people and the python. Many python owners don't give the python the care it needs.

Snake Bites

In 1992, a hurricane ruined a snake **facility** near Everglades National Park. About 800 python babies escaped into the park.

Pythons have become an **invasive species** in the Florida Everglades. People dump their pet pythons in this habitat. This hurts other animals living there.

Protecting Pythons

Pythons are some of the longest snakes in the world. They have a deadly squeeze and super strength. What can people do to keep these awesome creatures alive? It's important to keep python habitats safe from construction and **deforestation**. It's also important to spread the word about the dangers of the python pet trade.

Will a python attack a person? Not usually. Luckily, pythons would much rather hunt animals than people. They just want to hunt in peace!

Glossary

constrictor: A snake that winds around and squeezes prey.

defense: A feature of a living thing that helps keep it safe.

deforestation: The act or result of cutting down or burning all the trees in an area.

digest: To break down food inside the body so the body can use it.

facility: Buildings that are built for a certain purpose.

habitat: The natural place where an animal or plant lives.

identify: To tell what something is.

invasive species: Plants or animals from one area that spread quickly in a new area and harm native plants and animals.

mammal: A warm-blooded animal that has a backbone and hair, breathes air, and feeds milk to its young.

prey: An animal hunted by other animals for food.

species: A group of plants or animals that are all the same kind.

venomous: Having a poisonous bite.

Index

A

Africa, 10
African rock python, 4, 7
anacondas, 4
Australia, 10

B

ball python, 7
birds, 14, 16
Burmese python, 4, 5, 6, 8, 11

C

China, 10
crocodiles, 14, 16

D

deer, 16

E

eggs, 8
Europe, 10
Everglades, 20, 21

F

Florida, 21

I

India, 10

J

Jacobson's organ, 12

L

lizards, 14

M

mammals, 14, 16

P

pigs, 16
predators, 4, 9, 14, 16
prey, 4, 6, 12, 16, 18
Pythonidae, 4

R

reticulated python, 4, 6, 7
rodents, 16

T

tongue, 12, 13

U

United States, 10

Websites

Due to the changing nature of Internet links, PowerKids Press has developed an online list of websites related to the subject of this book. This site is updated regularly. Please use this link to access the list: www.powerkidslinks.com/soth/pyth